A Zebra

by Ethan Cruz
illustrated by Rusty Fletcher

Core Decodable 70

Bothell, WA • Chicago, IL • Columbus, OH • New York, NY

MHEonline.com

Copyright © 2015 McGraw-Hill Education

All rights reserved. No part of this publication may be reproduced or distributed in any form or by any means, or stored in a database or retrieval system, without the prior written consent of McGraw-Hill Education, including, but not limited to, network storage or transmission, or broadcast for distance learning.

Send all inquiries to:
McGraw-Hill Education
8787 Orion Place
Columbus, OH 43240

ISBN: 978-0-02-132407-1
MHID: 0-02-132407-7

Printed in the United States of America.

2 3 4 5 6 7 8 9 DOC 20 19 18 17 16 15

We made a recent visit to a ranch.
We visited these horses.

These horses have a big secret.
A zebra runs with them.

But which is the zebra?
These horses will not tell.

We looked and looked all over.
But we did not even get a hint.

So has the zebra left?
Or is he just well hidden?

For the time being, we cannot tell.
Can you spot a zebra?